DARK PSYCHOLOGY SECRETS

Uncover the secrets to defend yourself against mind control, deception, narcissism, brainwashing. How to Become the Owner of Your Life and stop being manipulated.

JOHN DARK

TABLE OF CONTENT

DARK 1
PSYCHOLOGY 1
Chapter 1 9

Understanding Deception 9

Theories, Taxonomies, and Frameworks 14
Taxonomy in Psychological Space 16

Chapter 2 18

Deception 18
Tactics 18

Following an Unreasonable Request by a More
Reasonable One 18
Making an Unusual Request Prior to Making the Actual
Request 19
Instilling Fear and Relief 19
Making the Deceived Party Feel Guilty 20
Usage of Bribery 20
Playing the Victim 21
Using of Logic 22
Not Breaking of Character 23

Chapter 3 25

Deception 25
Spectrum 25
TYPES OF DECEPTION 25

LIES 26
EQUIVOCATIONS 26
CONCEALMENTS 26
EXAGGERATION 27
UNDERSTATEMENTS 27
Honing of Manipulation Skills 27
TAKING ACTING CLASSES 27
LEARNING TO READ PEOPLE 28

TARGETS OF MANIPULATION 28

Chapter 4 31

Accepting 31
Reality 31

Chapter 5 35

Psychologists.. 35
Actions 35
Beyond Deceptions 35

Chapter 6 41

What to Do.. 41
When 41
Deception Occurs.................................... 41

Chapter 7 47

Ways to Overcome Disappointment.................... 47
SCREAM IT 47

Acquire a Broader Focus............................ *48*
Understand Who You Are *49*
Practice Acceptance *50*
Ignore Criticism *51*
Think Big... *51*
Allow Your Timeline to Be a Dot *52*
Hear It from Others *52*

CHAPTER 8 55

Critical Issues...................................... 55
for a Good 55
and Powerful life and................................ 55
Successful Career 55

Have a Good Character *55*
Be Creative....................................... *56*
Develop a Positive Image.......................... *57*
Maintain a Positive Attitude....................... *57*
Embrace the Right Work Habits *58*
Have Contact...................................... *59*

Chapter 9 61

How to Deal 61
with 61
Manipulative People................................. 61

Ignoring Them... 61
Believe Your Judgment 62
Never Compromise...62
Don't Ask for their Permission.....................................63
Have a Purpose 63
Be Responsible for Yourself 64
Don't Fit In..65

Chapter 10 .... **66**

The Basics 66
of 66
Brainwashing 66

Brainwashing Techniques: 66

HOW NOT TO BE BRAINWASHED: 72

It is not the strongest of the species that survives, nor the most intelligent that survives. It is the one that is most adaptable to change. 76

Chapter 11 77

The Process 77
of 77
Brainwashing 77

Preparation 77
Vulnerable Condition 78
The Elements 79
The Leader 80
The Followers 80
The Process 81

Chapter 12.. **84**

Case Studies of...84
Dark Psychology: 84
Joseph Stalin,...84
Adolf Hitler, ...84
And..84
Charles Manson 84

Adolf Hitler 85
Joseph Stalin 86

Charles Manson..*87*

Chapter 13...**89**

Brainwashing Tricks That Work with Anyone, Even the Smartest..89

Subliminal Brainwashing in Films.........................*89*
Sense of Belonging *90*
Repetition and Reprogramming *91*
Imitation..*93*
Use of Rituals...*94*

Chapter 14 ....**96**

Dark Triad..96

How to Identify Dark Triad Traits..................... *97*

Chapter 15...**99**

What Is the...99
Dark Triad?...99

Causes of the Dark Triad *100*
Machiavellianism......................................*102*
Characteristics of Machiavellian Individuals............*102*
Narcissism *105*
Characteristics of Narcissists *105*
Psychopathy *107*
Characteristics of Psychopaths...................... *107*

CHAPTER 1

UNDERSTANDING DECEPTION

The act of lying is a common phenomenon in the world. There are several reasons why people chose to be deceptive in their day-to-day lives. The act of deception can be done either for personal gain or ideological reasons. The act is very dangerous because it has the potential to harm the victim. The process is always carried for a varied period that is considered by the person performing it. In fact, the act of deception is broad because it can be done without necessarily harming the victim being lied to.

There are several ways an individual can choose to understand what deception is. The best way to begin the process of deep understanding commences with knowing the definition of the term. The act of deception can be described as a process of making a person believe something that is not true. It entails a broad form of making a false reality through the manipulation of appearances. The current world has seen and experienced several forms of deceptions in several contexts. Therefore, it becomes a difficult task to categorize these forms of deception using a common feature in them. This is despite every act of deception, having a familiar resemblance to the others.

Deception contains both forms of simulation and dissimulation. Simulation is the act of withholding or hiding vital information from the victim of the deceitful act. On the other hand, dissimulation is the process of putting out misleading or wrong information to an individual being deceived. Both acts of lying can be done by either commission or omission of information. However, the moral compass seems to support deception that is achieved by omission rather than that of commission.

The first group of psychologists that studied the art of deception did their research in the year 1989. They did their study by looking at sleight of hand magic or conjuring as their paradigm. Conjuring can be described as one of the acts in the world that an individual's ability to deceive is its success domain. However, this form of deception has a significant difference from that made by a confident person or a spy agent. It is because it has an element of a sanctioned form of deception. The person performing conjuring has a contract with his or her audience to fool the people watching him or her. Therefore, an individual would not be described as a good magician in events he or she fails to fool the audience. Also, the parties experiencing conjuring are always aware they are about to be fooled prior to the action.

However, the act of deception has a different way its success

comes about. During the act of deception, the victims are not told or made aware of what is taking place or what is about to happen. Several magic tricks have been accepted by the current world. On the other hand, there are close to no forms of deceptions that have been sanctioned by the global society. It is because several communities across the globe have their moral compass conflicting with the act of lying. This is despite some forms of lying being tolerated and being sanctions among some groups of people. These forms of sanctioned lies include fantasies, fables, and jokes since they cause little or no harm to society.

There are numerous depictions of deception and the context they have been used across the globe. There are moments or certain moments that teens or adolescents have been able to fool adults. The case does not occur only during teens or adolescents; there are several cases that varied people of different ages and sex have been able to lie to doctors or other health practitioners. They would aim to avoid or change the prescriptions that they are given. Consumer Fraud in the health industry has been among the common case that has been highlighted in the current world.

The other form of deception that has been highlighted for a long time is known as military and strategic deception. This form of deception has been practiced from time immemorial by several communities or nations across the globe. Ploy and feints are very important and highly valued in sports and games as forms of deception. People such as gambling cheats, impersonators, and fraudulent psychics have increased in numbers across the world. This has made swindles and games of confidence taking a common fall on victims who are willing.

The criminal case of deception is commonly known as a forgery in various countries in the global village. Several people have drawn their interest in knowing and understanding deception. This has seen publications such as books and journals focusing on plagiarism and other deceptive forms that are in the scientific field. The other form of deception that has seen a rise in interests from sociobiologists, psychologists, and philosophers is known as self-deception.

These forms of deceptions are worth being looked at. However, the primary focus is being put at face to face deception that entails two people communicating. This has led to several types of research in the psychology of a human being. Several people are curious to know how to deceive other people or how to know the moments they are being deceived by other people. Such forms of deceptions are prone to occur when there is an actual exchange of information between people. It is determined by factors such as psychological issues and structural matters.

Life is 10% **what happens to you and** 90% **how you react to it**.

(Charles R. Swindoll)

THEORIES, TAXONOMIES, AND FRAMEWORKS

Several scientists tried to develop the psychology of deception in the late 19th century. They supported their research with the paradigm of conjuring as the case for deception. This research aimed at classifying the general principles that are used in conjuring while mystifying the audience. This will then form a base to explain the framework the act of deception acts on. However, conjuring could not for the best paradigm because they are different acts, as noted above.

Therefore, this has led to the development of taxonomies to work as the framework for the theory of deception. A good taxonomy helps to contribute to the development of a theory that is adequate. This is made possible because taxonomy helps in directing the focus of an individual to a specific study. The first step of conducting taxonomy involves considering the process as extremely tentative. There are certain challenging circumstances that can be experienced during the process of a research survey. These challenges include; some categories will lack representatives, and there will be other forms of study that will have difficulties fitting into these categories. However, a good taxonomy exercise is

judged by its ability to help its users.

Several taxonomies on deception have been developed by several theorists. These taxonomies have a critical advantage to the current and preceding generation. It is because they will be used as a source of developing comprehensive deception systems in the current and preceding generation. These systems can be pivotal in helping future investigations on deceptions. However, the most important aim of taxonomies is helping to develop scientific theories of deception.

Such a theory will have several components in it. It will comprise of basic variables, common concepts, and laws that will allow an individual to understand deception. The successful forms of taxonomies have been able to start with the actual definition of what deception is. It goes deeper into more scientific explanations of the phenomenon. These analyses take common cases that occur in the daily life of humans to be able to relate what people understanding of the concept.

TAXONOMY IN PSYCHOLOGICAL SPACE

During this taxonomy, a systematic relationship between the terms of deceptions and English speakers was studied. This study entails how forty-six terms were being related to

deception. There were several theories that were invoked theories of deception that were acknowledged. Deception can encompass categories such as lies, masks, crimes, fiction, and plays. The forms of deceptions that have been practiced across the world tend to have a clear line of similarities among them. This form of taxonomy is very hierarchal. It is because the six categories can be grouped under two major categories.

The two major categories that characterize the six categories of deception are known as exploitative fabrications and benign fabrications. There are several things that are encompassed in benign fabrications, which include playing and fiction. On the other hand, exploitative fabrications involve several activities such as underlies, masks, crimes, and lies. This taxonomy was a spearhead of two individuals during the 1980s. They were Mr. Hopper and Mr. Bell who went further to try looking into the forms of deceptions that are morally acceptable, harmless and socially acceptable; and morally unacceptable, harmful and socially unacceptable as new categories of deception taxonomy.

The first dimension was labeled as harmfulness. This dimension entails forms of deception that ranged from immoral, bad, harmful, and unacceptable. The terms used in dimension were termed as low rating words. High-rated terms were used to describe harmless, moral, and acceptable. The second dimension was labeled as covertness. The items on this dimension were rated highly based on convert, nonverbal, and indirect use—those who were rated lowly were based on verbal, direct, and covert.

CHAPTER 2

DECEPTION

TACTICS

The current world has seen several forms of deceptions that have been done. These activities have been done at home, work, and several social places. The common view from the vast global society puts this act as immoral.

FOLLOWING AN UNREASONABLE REQUEST BY A MORE REASONABLE ONE

This tactic is used by several people who deceive others to get what they want. It can be described as a time-tested tactic of deception. If an individual does want to perform the act of deception, he or she is likely to make an unreasonable request as first. The unreasonable always has a high chance of being rejected. It is then followed by the second request, which tends to sound appealing to the target if compared to the earlier demand. This form of tactic has been used several times in the cooperate world. The best depiction can be seen when there is an involvement of actual buying and selling of goods or services.

MAKING AN UNUSUAL REQUEST PRIOR TO MAKING THE ACTUAL REQUEST

The other way to make an individual do a task for you is by making unusual forms of requests. These kinds of requests can make an individual be swept away by being caught off guard while the request is being made. During these moments, it is always difficult for an individual to reject the request being made. However, going direct to the request creates an avenue where the individual's needs have a high possibility of facing rejection right away. A good depiction can be used in a street if one needs to tie his or her shoe; he

or she can first go-ahead to show the target that he/she has a sprained back then go on to fix his/her shoes.

INSTILLING FEAR AND RELIEF

The process of deception entails an individual getting what he or she wants. This can be achieved when the target is first made to fear the worst. The second step involves making the person relieved by giving a better option. This makes the individual happy as such would be in a strong position to grant the person deceiving him or her whatever he or she wants. What this technique entail is a little bit of trick in getting the result desired.

MAKING THE DECEIVED PARTY FEEL GUILTY

Guilt is a very deep form of emotion that is very critical in one's life. It is one of the most used tactics when people are manipulated into doing certain things. The first step involves picking the right target to perform this technique on. Most individuals who are selected are those who are prone to feeling guilty most of the time. The second step is about ensuring the target selected is guilty about what the deceiving party wants. These individuals could be business partners who have denied an individual a deal; it can also be a parent or a friend. One way a friend can be deceived is by being reminding them of favors made by them to the deceiving party.

USAGE OF BRIBERY

Bribery is a common occurrence that is being witnessed across the world. It is described as one of the best ways an individual carrying out deceit can achieve his or her act of manipulation. Bribery can be described as an act of offering another party something valuable in exchange with a form of favor. Valuables, in this case, can be money or other forms of offers. During the act of bribery, an individual conducting the act of deceit does not have to black his or her target.

The process is handled with finesse for it to be successful. The first step involves an individual researching on the most important values his or her party is in deer need of. People tend to be very desperate when they need certain things urgently that are way out of their reach. The second step involves the party practicing the manipulative act, not making his or her action look obvious. They tend to make their actions seem like a form of assistance to the other party so as to hide their main intentions.

PLAYING THE VICTIM

Playing the victim during the act of deceit has the potential of making the act successful. The process has its advantage, though—during deception, one needs to be careful so he/she doesn't go overboard. This makes the tactic to be used during precise moments and sparingly. The tactic is meant to hit the heart of the targeted victim. The manipulators tend to act in a way that depicts them as altruistic and wonderful people.

This is then followed by a deceiving act, making you see that everything is crumbling around them. They tend to play dumb during the process and act pitifully.

USING OF LOGIC

This technique works better on certain group of people. The category includes those who are predicted to have a rational frame of mind. These kinds of people tend to be easily persuaded with logical thinking. Therefore, manipulators tend to have at least three reasons to try convincing the target. These reasons tend to have advantages for both the manipulator and the target. These thoughts are always presented in a rational form to help the manipulator not to lose his or her cool. During these presentations, emotions tend to be drawn away for the manipulator to be able to reach his or her target mind.

NOT BREAKING OF CHARACTER

This is a trick that nearly every successful manipulator practices. There are certain moments that a manipulator can be suspected by people or a person around him or her. During such moments, a person conducting his or her deceiving act cannot accept or admit to his or her actions. They are prone to turning the situation to the other party that had discovered them. It is because the process of deceiving a person the second time is hard if they had learned of one's actions earlier on.

You never change things by fighting the existing reality. To change something, build a new model that makes the existing model obsolete.

(Buckminster Fuller)

CHAPTER 3

DECEPTION

SPECTRUM

The spectrum of deception can be narrowed into three main components that an individual does need to know. There are several types of deceptions, several targets of deceptions, and ways that techniques of deceptions are enhanced.

TYPES OF DECEPTION

Types of deceptions can be grouped into five forms that are common across the world. These sets include understatements, equivocations, and concealments.

LIES

This form of deception has been commonly practiced across the world. It entails an individual giving out or providing false information to his or her target.

EQUIVOCATIONS

This form of deception entails an individual carrying out the manipulation process making ambiguous or vague statements to his or her victim.

CONCEALMENTS

Concealment is a very sloppy form of deception. It is often referred to as deception by omission. This is because there is certainly critica

information that is normally left out from the information given to the target.

EXAGGERATION

During the performance of this type of deception, the truth is often stretched. This can be described as the opposite of understatements,

UNDERSTATEMENTS

The truth is always downplayed during the practice of this act. What was meant to be the truth is always undersold to the target of deception.

HONING OF MANIPULATION SKILLS

TAKING ACTING CLASSES

The act of manipulation greatly depends on an individual's ability, being able to control his or her emotions. This entails being able to make the target of deception to be receptive to the contrived feelings. Taking classes in acting always has a huge benefit in helping an individual use various emotional techniques. It also helps an individual to improve his or her persuasion skills. Classes in acting can be enhanced with a manipulator being taught by a master in the act of deception.

LEARNING TO READ PEOPLE

People are generally different. This means that every person in the world is different psychologically and emotionally. Therefore, every person has different ways he or she is supposed to be manipulated. Before the act of deception is made, a manipulator takes his or her time to study his or her target's emotional or psychological weakness. There are people who are very emotional, there are others who have strong reflexes on guilt, and there are others who are more receptive to a rational approach.

TARGETS OF MANIPULATION

There are several people in the world who are targets of manipulation. This means that anyone is likely to be manipulated in his or her life as a child, adolescent, or adult. Friends can be manipulated by people who they refer to as friends. The process of deceiving friends can be among the hardest forms of deception. However, there are several cases that its success has been seen or witnessed. The steps used are similar to those that are being used by a manipulator to his or her partner. The first step entails an individual using floods of emotion to capture his or her target. The second step involves reminding them of the favors done to them and laying guilt on them. Other people who are prone to deception include bosses, business partners, parents, teachers, and doctors.

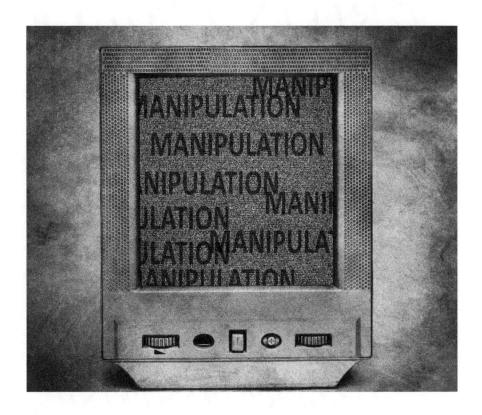

THERE IS A DRIVING FORCE MORE POWERFUL THAN STEAM, ELECTRICITY AND NUCLEAR POWER: THE WILL.

(ALBERT EINSTEIN)

CHAPTER 4

ACCEPTING

REALITY

Accepting reality is seeing and knowing what your life is like and learning to embrace that fact. Reality helps us see life as it is and not as a fragment of fiction. It helps one get out of their imaginary daze. This is very important for everyone to take up. Reality enables you to plan for the future, as you already know where you stand and where you want to go. Hence, reality is seen to be critical to human growth. So how does one identify and learn to accept the reality that he or she is living in?

The first step to accepting reality is learning to support yourself as you understand what your reality is. This is what we say, going through the learning process with the right mindset. This is where every step you take, you need to appreciate yourself since it is not easy going forward. It takes effort and hard work. Some say it is easy to go back, but the effort you take going forward is to be much appreciated. So, every small step is to be taken positively no matter how small since it took so much energy to take that step.

The other is taking things less personally. This means listening less to negative comments that people give. The only thing that these negative comments do is to make you see yourself as inferior and insignificant. They push you back and make you doubt yourself. This is very bad for any progress you might have made. So, what are you supposed to do with these negative comments that keep flying in your way? The fact is you should know yourself and keep that always in mind. What you should do is loosen up a little and live life to the fullest.

Another way is by taking things slow, taking one step at a time. That means going slowly. Do not push yourself too hard since progress should be a slow activity. Go with the rhythm of how you feel. Make sure that your body soul and mind give you permission for the next step you take. Know that it is not a race and give yourself maximum understanding. Know when to start something new and when to take a pause if that's what you want or need. The point is to listen to yourself at all times.

Finally, get used to people and things as they are. Learn to know that people are different. Accept that they are different and that it's not changing. Also, learn that things are the way they are since that is just how life is. Do not force things—just let things be and let yourself be what you are. Know that you are the one to accept things if you are going to fit in. So, this is something that you should know. Also, learn the art of compromising with people and all that makes the world. These are just but a few tips to take in accepting reality.

Yesterday I was clever, so I wanted to change the world. Today I am wise, so I am changing myself.

Gialal al-Din Rumi

CHAPTER 5

PSYCHOLOGISTS

ACTIONS

BEYOND DECEPTIONS

Before I rush off to discuss what this chapter holds, I will let you understand what it means. It may seem difficult in perception. All this chapter is looking at is the ethics that psychologists use during their work. There are several, including deception, but in this chapter, it is being excluded in the discussion. Some might ask how is deception even an ethic used? This question has been circling a lot of people's minds. It has been a cause of debate, as we have all taken deception in a negative form. There are obvious reasons why it is taken as a cause of action by a psychologist. It is believed that in order to catch a liar, then you must be a liar, too. This statement makes us see the use of deception. Hence, psychologists believe and follow this statement. This is a way to lure the deceiver. Making him or her comfortable in opening up is their main goal. They just know that this is the easiest and fastest way to convince these people to talk about their truth. This method may seem kind of sketchy, but there is a reasonable explanation for its use. Apart from deception, what are the other ways psychologists take action?

The first is being confidential with their patients. To gain someone's trust, you must be able to keep his or her secrets. So, for a psychologist, this is the number one priority once they take up on a patient. Confidentiality means that all that a patient says to you should remain between you and him or her. This is like rule number one for all counseling sessions. It should feel like talking to a neutral person who is not judging you, and that is not allowed to spill your guts in front of other people. This enables one to express themselves fully allowing

the psychologist to see through you. This is meant to help you become better from your problem or issue. The psychologist does not write anything down unless the patient permits it. This is something that comes with the confidentiality package in a psychologist domain.

If there was any breach of trust, then one can be sure that his or her information was not kept privately. A psychologist that uses these methods of dealing with things leads to massive success. That means trust is built, then the truth is said, and action is finally taken to help the patient.

The other is getting consent from the patient. The psychologist is just like a guide on this journey. They are just there to lead. They do not make any decisions for the patient. What they do is give some suggestions which the patient has to pick out. The way forward is to be dictated by the patient. The pace to be taken too is to be said by the patient. The driver in therapy is always the patient and not the psychologist. The patient is to choose what he or she wants at the end of therapy. All of these factors are to be considered.

The psychologist is to ask for permission every time he or she wants to bring in something new to the table. This is important since it is the recovery of the patient and not the psychologist. The patient knows what is best for him or her through the psychologist's guidance. The patient should also take his or her time without being rushed. The psychologist's work is to listen and give advice. He or she cannot change the patient. The change should be consulted with the patient. Overall, the patient is the word.

Also, there is the right to step aside or withdraw from the case. A psychologist has a right to refer you to someone else if need be. That may be because of the close relationship between you and them—also, the closeness between you and a former patient of his or hers. There also is the fact that he or she will be unable to deal with the situation that is presented to him or her. If he or she thinks that it is in his best interest to put the patient in someone else's good care—this is

important, even if it looks insignificant. The psychologist reviews the patient's case and sees what option is best for him or her. The psychologist is able to see whether he or she is the right person for this patient. Turning down a patient is very ethical for any psychologist. This withdrawal should have an excellent explanation since this is a show of professionalism. This is another ethical doing of people in the field of psychology. It does not show a lack of knowledge—it just shows where some are good and where they are not. It is the responsibility of the psychologist to choose wisely.

The final thing is protecting their clients. This is supposed to be something that is done during and after therapy. The patient becomes a psychologist's life too. That means all that is going on in the patient's life is the psychologist's business. This means the mental, physical, and psychological health is in that bracket. He or she should get to know the patient's life and how it is, in general. He or she should know his family and friends in character. This helps to figure the root cause of the problem and in finding a suitable solution for the problem. They are supposed to be the support system of the patient during and after recovery. The after recovery is important to avoid issues of the patient going back to old habits. There are so many more ethical ways in which psychologists' take action, but these are just some of them. These are the pointers for the others. These are just beside the use of deception. We have seen how each plays its own role in therapy. That is in the life of the psychologist and the patient himself or herself. I hope these gave you the limelight to other actions used in psychology.

Whatever you can do or dream you can, begin it. Boldness has genius, power and magic in it. Begin it.

Johan Wolfgang von Goethe

CHAPTER 6

WHAT TO DO

WHEN

DECEPTION OCCURS

Deception occurs every day of our lives, so what are we supposed to do? Deception can occur at work, in school, and even at home. This is something that we cannot easily escape from in our lives. It crosses through our social lives just like that. There has been a discussion about deception everywhere around the globe. It happens with most people, so how do we deal with it? Do we run from it? Do we fight it? What happens next in all this frenzy?

The first thing to do is to note the deception. You cannot handle something that you cannot see for yourself. Note how you were deceived and by whom. It seems like a silly step, but this is the main step to be taken. Deep inside, look at how things went down. Look at the sly and cunning things the deceiver might have done at the point of deception. These small details are the key to you knowing how and when you were deceived—since this is the first thing to do. How does one know that they were deceived by someone? The first thing to remember is that the story might be shady.

Another thing to know is that the person has to be sly for deception to work. So, listen to the story carefully as you look for the discrepancies. As you move on with your search note sly or cunning aspects of people. These aspects are meant to lead you to know whether someone is deceptive with you in any way. These are the first things that are considered during an issue that involves deception. This step is what leads to others. The success of this one makes the others easy to deal with as they come.

The next step is finding out the reason why people are deceptive. What is their motivation? This is the question that comes to mind. When you find out, what was the deception? There is always a reason behind everything. This is no less for deception. There is that factor that leads someone to indulge in this terrible vice that exists. Find out whether it is just a growing habit on someone that they started and cannot stop. This is possible. This is what we call an addiction to lies and deceptions. This is usually for the advance deceivers. This is also why some keep doing it to get out of trouble. You lie so that you avoid getting punished or criticized. This usually a major cause or motivation that people have to be deceptive. This cause can make you do a lot of things you did not expect to do. There is also another cause, which is where someone wants something, and they can only get it through deception.

This is also another major motivation for the deception of other people. This helps us to understand the reasons for it.

Confront the deceptive person once you know who and why they deceived you, go and talk to them. Do not wait or say, let it pass. You, as the victim, have to find out why they behaved like that with you. Find out whether it's their habit, and that is something that they cannot stop doing. Confront them not too strongly or harshly. This is to enable you to get the information you want in the end. If you are harsh, you will scare them that they will be afraid to tell you anything. The point is not to scare them off—the point is to make them talk. Make them feel comfortable, as well as a little bit intimidated so that they can spill the truth. Warn them about this vice that they are doing and give them some advice to lead them to the right path. The right path that they should have been on in the first place. Make a friend out of them and be there for them during the transition process of them leaving the world of deception and lies. These are things to be followed step by step if you really want to make a great difference.

Take action at any social institution where you see any kind of deception taking place. This means speaking up and making people aware of this bad vice. Also, there is knowing what steps or measures to be taken when someone decides to deceive others. It means that this matter is not to be handled lightly. It should be taught at home, in school, in all places that involve people interacting with each other. It can happen anywhere, and it should not be taken like a joke or something close to that. People who have undergone deception should have a place of refuge where they can recover from the trauma. The point is finding the voice for the victims and

taking care of these deceivers. There should also be talks of why one should not take on deception into their lives. This all incorporated together should work for the better of the people. One should not work alone; one should rally up others for support whether moral, physical, or even economical. All this should be for the cause ahead and for making the world free of deceivers or chronic liars. This is a smart way to deal with the deceivers.

There are so many ways to change the world and to make it deception free. There is so much to deception, and I know most of you agree that it should be put to a stop. People should learn to be honest, no matter what happens. What matters is the thought. Honesty is usually the best policy anyone can follow. All we should do is try to live the example and be confident until we throw out what is called deception. The tips given are just but a few. There are many more, but for now, this is it. This should give you a mirror of the other tips.

CHAPTER 7

WAYS TO OVERCOME DISAPPOINTMENT

Disappointment being an emotional state can be built up through the sensory organs and mind via thoughts. Life usually provides multiple opportunities that people try to maximize on as a step towards different types of goals. When the level of preferred satisfaction is not achieved, depending on an individual, disappointment may creep in positively or negatively. Distress can be positive if one is already in control of factors causing it in the first place. The negative disappointment is, however, one that is to worry about. There have been ways to overcome these negative disappointments that have been developed over time and vary from conditions to individuals for them to work accordingly.

SCREAM IT

One of the greatest mistakes most people do is letting the disappointment sink below the waters of the mind. This only gives the case a chance to develop and combine into regrets and later depression. Letting it out has been seen to work at the early stages of life when kids are still improving emotional stability. Kids keep their laughs long as much as their cries are loud. This ensures their emotional experience is never hurried; thus, when something comes up, they are ready to move on.

It is always wise to allow yourself to feel with time, not being a constraint at any point. Trying to change the situations or sides in any scenario in most cases turns things sour before can incur more painful emotions. Giving this time and allowing for the experience to sink in will be more fruitful and will allow for healing later on.

ACQUIRE A BROADER FOCUS

Having a let your body treat itself like a partner now, it becomes possible to listen to other parties involved in your emotional status. In case you felt disappointed in someone, this will allow you to inquire about their involvement. Most times, it happens that those involved never knew that their actions upset you. Friends, for example, can make embarrassing comments assuming you are good with it without realizing the discomfort it brings. You might also understand someone disappointed you in a situation of their life where they are going through something sturdy and uneasy.

While this may be something similar to what you were going through, your other colleague may be denying themselves time to heal, leading to their relay behavior. Only by giving yourself some time to understand your emotions can you know and relate to someone else's behavior more easily.

UNDERSTAND WHO YOU ARE

Intense emotional experiences, such as disappointments, can cause strenuous effects on your emotional state. Some of the results of these include depression and self-denial. Understanding part of who you are, not only allows you to protect your pillars but also use them to your advantage.

Say, for example, a person with a kind heart. If such a person were to be hurt by someone, then s/he would choose to block such a quality towards a person who disappoints them. It would, however, be advisable to take a break and realize that such values protect you more times than they ever hurt back. With such resolutions and understanding, you would stick to your pillars and thus keep such memories from changing your life's path and personal definitions.

This process, in most times, will let you realize that whatever the feeling, it is restrained to time and eventually, change happens and everything changes. Over time one learns the stretch to which such emotional experiences can take them and thus obtains trust and belief in their ability to cope with external factors as they watch every sunset in their life.

Character is higher than intellect. A great soul will be strong to live as well as think.

Ralph Waldo Emerson

PRACTICE ACCEPTANCE

As part of our psychological behavior, humans are easily inclined to deflect negative emotional experiences to avoid inflicting pain on their minds. As a result, humans withdraw when the skills get tough, thus placing the weight of frustrations on everyone's shoulder or just anybody, to offload it off theirs. By regularly accepting the results and blowback of our involvement in them, you more acknowledge the uncertainty in perfection and lets you take the flaws in others and yourself. This will allow you to see the beauty in life and uniqueness in people's character and behavior.

IGNORE CRITICISM

You may have noticed that, in most times, when you take a shot at doing something you are passionate about, your results end up being criticized by other people. It is impossible to control what other people choose to say. You may order people to cease speaking ideas, but then communication is more than just verbal. It is best advisable to keep your lane clear of such negative energy, and this might give you the room you need to excel in.

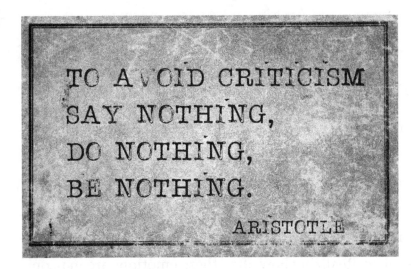

TO AVOID CRITICISM
SAY NOTHING,
DO NOTHING,
BE NOTHING.

ARISTOTLE

THINK BIG

Thinking everything is part of something bigger will let you keep your head high even when you fall several times? It helps you believe everything is part of something with a bigger significance. This will allow you to understand that disappointments are probably meant to occur at some point to help you relay back your original energy to your venture and core spirit of your undertakings. This will also let you believe that your general idea is too big to fail after minor shortcomings allowing you to hold onto even the last inch of it.

ALLOW YOUR TIMELINE TO BE A DOT

Letting yourself believe that what is happening is a dot in a bigger plan will allow you to keep up in a positive momentum as you await your overall picture to come to life. The spirit of something beautiful at the end of it all will let you tune every step to be better than the last in an attempt to outdo yourself.

HEAR IT FROM OTHERS

Sometimes, lessons can be learned through others. By listening to other people in the same situations, you understand how necessary such experiences can be and start to comprehend their recovery. Group talks can help one come into agreement with their situations and begin recovery sooner. Realizing how often these emotions are in people's lives, it helps you feel less segregated and more of a member in everyone's life and experiences. You can also learn of recovery procedures from different people, you would immediately, or eventually come to discover one that works for you.

Staying hopeful for a better tomorrow will always keep your pupils wide open. As Philosopher St. Thomas Aquinas said, "To hope for something is to claim its significance to us, and so to claim ourselves."

Like everything else, disappointment is part of emotional experience and with that allows us to better ourselves and our relations with others, making it more realistic and natural. Like everything else, disappointment is part of emotional experience and with that will enable us to better ourselves and our relationships with others.

Have the courage to follow your heart and intuition. They somehow already know what you truly want to become. Everything else is secondary.

Steve Jobs

CHAPTER 8

CRITICAL ISSUES FOR A GOOD AND POWERFUL LIFE AND SUCCESSFUL CAREER

Do not spend your entire life wondering how to achieve success, you need to give yourself time to figure that out. You can be successful both in life and in your career. All you need to do is have focus and maintain a positive attitude towards everything. There are several essential issues you can apply in life to achieve this goal. Some of the approaches to use to live a good life and have a compelling career include:

HAVE A GOOD CHARACTER

Having a desirable trait will open opportunities for you and will earn you respect. When you embrace integrity, you will gain trust, and people will believe you. Your character will improve your health as well as your career. Honesty, as well as self-discipline, is what defines a person's real nature. To have a strong foundation of anything in life, you need to be a trustworthy person. A good character will make people believe in you and trust that you can keep your word. Following your words to the latter will make people entrust you and use you as a path to achieve their goals. You cannot be successful without the help of the people around you. They have to trust you so that they can use you to achieve success, and in the process, you will gain power. Your good trait will make you live in harmony with people, which will guarantee a happy life.

BE CREATIVE

For you to take a step forward in life, creativity must be part of you. If you want to achieve your targets within your set date, you have to be more creative. Having a great idea is not enough if you do not allow yourself to be creative. You will desire to search for better in a faster and natural way. You also need to think of the most affordable ways to implement that idea. All these with no creativity will not yield results. You can

attain wealth with a single plan when you incorporate creativity. Creativity will take you miles ahead in terms of your career and as well help you live a good life. Use the skills that you pose to improve quality as well as quantity. Seek to learn and have the experience, and you can predict the results and achieve them in a short time.

DEVELOP A POSITIVE IMAGE

Positivity matters a lot in the way you will live and whether you will be successful in your career. Your outside appearance is the basis that people will use to judge you. Take your time to make yourself look attractive, and you will attract people as well. Having interactions with people more often is what will open up doors for your career. Through such communications, you can get new ideas that never crossed your mind and think of implementing them. How you dress determines the kind of people you are likely to influence. Dressing well and decently will attract a lot of people who can help you move forward in life. You need to dress while aiming for success. People can go to the extent of criticizing you by how you look. Present yourself in an ideal way, and you will create the right image. It is worth investing time as well as resources to work on your outward appearance.

MAINTAIN A POSITIVE ATTITUDE

Develop a positive mental way of thinking of how to cut down the time to implement or set your goals. A positive attitude will elevate your career and give you a chance to live life to its fullest. No matter what you are going through, either good or bad, you have to look at things from a positive point of view.

Make good out of the bad, and you have an assurance to living a happy life. The ability you have to look at things in a different way when they are not moving in the right direction is what will make you successful. Be an optimistic person and

have confidence, and you will have the best life that you desire. The right mental attitude is vital in personal as well as professional experience.

EMBRACE THE RIGHT WORK HABITS

When you have desirable work habits, you will end up being more productive. Being productive will help you to climb up the ladder in your career. You will achieve more in the shortest time possible. Organize your work and be careful about how you go along with your daily activities. The right work ethics will help you meet your deadlines, which will translate to increased work output. Thinking and at the same taking action will be of importance. Before you begin any task, you need to write down all the ideas that you have and make priorities on the important ones to start implementing. You cannot be successful if you don't consider the likely shortcomings, the consequences and how to deal with them to reduce or eliminate the effect completely

HAVE CONTACT

No man is an island, and everyone needs people to prosper and have a good life. You need to have a significant number of connections and make sure they are people who can be of help to you. It takes time as well as efforts to have contacts and cultivate a network of healthy friendships. Having people who are always there for you and willing to support you is a great deal. You need to put in more effort when it comes to maintaining such circles so that you will move forward. People are likely to fuel changes that will occur in your life. The more you are known and loved by a significant number of people, the more likely you will have a pleasant experience. At any opportunity that you get, grab it to expand your network and do that continually. Your success is related to the number of people you know and is willing to help you.

CHAPTER 9

HOW TO DEAL

WITH

MANIPULATIVE PEOPLE

A manipulative person tries to use different approaches to get what they want from a person. They will make you feel guilty and then squeeze you using your kindness. You need to arm yourself with the skills to deal with such a person. Do not feel obliged to help them in any way, and don't follow their instructions. Remain calm, firm, and assertive in case of a disagreement with them. You need to have limits and make sure you do not spend much of your time with them, if possible. Steps to take while dealing with manipulative people include:

IGNORING THEM

Trying to pay attention to a manipulative person will make you fall into their trap more easily. Such a person will frustrate and confuse you to make sure they pick a fight with you. They will try to make you feel emotional so they can see you annoyed. They will influence you once they know what triggers your emotions. Ignore them and if possible, avoid them and do not involve them in your issues. Cut them entirely from your life. When it comes to a person that you cannot prevent, agree with what they have to say but do not do precisely that. Do what you believe is the right thing you need to do.

BELIEVE YOUR JUDGMENT

Do not give a manipulative person the chance to define you no matter what. You are the only one who has the right to identify yourself. You should trust yourself. That will make you the winner separating you from the losers. Have what you believe in and hold on to that while making sure that they do not affect your life.

NEVER COMPROMISE

Guilt is an emotion that should not disturb you when dealing with a manipulative person. The manipulator will use the guilt you feel to suppress you. They will do anything possible to make you guilty for the smallest of mistakes that you make. They also use your happiness as well as confidence to make you liable. Do not let self-doubt creep in since that is also a tool that people can use to manipulate you. When you are uncertain, a manipulator will try to gain power and bring you down. They will have more influence over you when you become doubtful. Make sure you do not compromise on your goals and values. Don't feel guilty or have self-doubt and keep in mind that you don't owe your manipulator anything. Be proud of the person you are and your achievements. You will destroy your happiness if you compromise, and that is not morally upright.

DON'T ASK FOR THEIR PERMISSION

Asking for permission before you do anything shows the presence of morals in you. Regardless of that, do not ask for permission from a manipulative person. People will try to manipulate you when you beg for permission to do anything. You have the right to take any action that you think is right without asking for a go-ahead from such a person. Take control of your life and choose what to do and at what time.

HAVE A PURPOSE

If you have no purpose in life, you give a manipulator chance to manipulate you more. You need to know that you are not where you are by mistake, or you were lucky to get yourself there. Living a life without purpose will make you believe in anything which should not be the case. You will get yourself doing anything since nothing matters to you. When you lack purpose, a manipulator will control you by feeding you unnecessary and useless information. When you have a purpose in life, a manipulator will not get a chance to hurt you. Have a focus, and they will not have control over you.

BE RESPONSIBLE FOR YOURSELF

Someone can fool you once, but do not give them a chance to fool you a second time. Do not act like a fool by giving a manipulator a chance to walk over you. Do not hold yourself but instead take good care of yourself in the best way possible. Understand that you are in charge of your happiness. Have self-awareness as well as self-respect and learn to say no to anyone who maltreats you.

Someone will manipulate you with your permission which may be indirect. If people think otherwise about you, that means you have permitted them to think that about you. You are responsible for your successes as well as failures, and you need to be accountable. Learning from your past mistakes is vital, and you should not trust people who hurt you over and over again. Surround yourself with people who will be of benefit to you rather than negative people.

DON'T FIT IN

Re-invent your time and again while you allow yourself not to fit into their ideas. Be different and embrace personal growth by defining yourself. Do not be consistent but be subject to change after a while. Your manipulator can be any person in your life. You can choose your friends, but you cannot define their character. Respond to manipulation in an active approach, and you will avoid getting hurt. If you lack wisdom, you might get into a fight with someone, which is not necessary at all. You need to detect when someone is manipulating you. Set clear boundaries and stand firm and don't let someone's mind or thoughts affect you. If they make a mistake, do not try to collect them. A manipulative person will do something for you and will in return demand you to repay them and complain if you fail to. Do not let anyone treat you as an option since you deserve the best treatment. If you are in a friendship where someone does not allow you to be yourself, dissolve that friendship since it is of no importance. Avoid any interactions with a manipulator and do not fall for their tricks. Set your goals, and it will be hard for someone to manipulate you when you have something to drive you. Do not let them have access to how you think or feel about anything.

CHAPTER 10

THE BASICS

OF

BRAINWASHING

Brainwashing occurs when a person's mind is being played with and controlled using various psychological techniques. To be able to brainwash a person, multiple steps need to be taken.

BRAINWASHING TECHNIQUES:

- **Isolation** - this involves keeping the victim away from anyone he/she knows, friends and family. This is done so the victim doesn't have multiple options available to him/her. With the victim's friends and family around, the victim will have multiple suggestions available to him/her which inturn make the attacks job difficult hence the need for isolation as then only the attackers suggestion and reasoning is available to the victim.

- **Identity assault** - this is a way of attacking a person's ego, which affects a person's identity. This brings confusion to a person so that he starts having questions like who he thinks he is, and what he believes in is attacked and he starts to have self-doubt which leads him to start questioning his real identity because he feels lesser as a person. An attacker will use this technique to induce self-doubt in their target.

- **Dependency on fear** - the victim is physically and psychologically tortured until fear is the only thing he/she has available to him/her. The victim has so much doubt that they believe there is no escape other than for them to oblige to what they are being told and forced to do. They are so scared that they cannot even share what they are going through with anyone else because they have been warned of the consequences that could befall them if they decided to betray the attacker.

- **Guilt** - here, the attacker makes the target feel guilty for everything they do. The victim will be made to think that he is the reason for various fails, big or small. The feeling of guilt will make the victim struggle with his/her identity, as they do not fully trust themselves, or are not confident in themselves, and therefore they will not be able to understand when they are carrying a guilt that they shouldn't otherwise be carrying.

The attacker is always relentless and would use any opportunity to take advantage of the victim. It may be a guilt attack on how they talk, what they believe in, who they are friends with or even how they look.

- **Self-betrayal** - when the victim has already lost his/her identity and carries a feeling of guilt, the next thing the attacker does is to make the victim drop his beliefs. He will be made to believe that his beliefs are worthless, and he has to distance himself from individuals who share the same beliefs. This means that people who have otherwise helped him become strangers because he has cut ties with them, and there is no way of communication. This will lead to more loss of the victim's identity because he has agreed to betray himself. Sometimes, it involves denouncing his family, and therefore there is no one to quicken him back to realizing what is really going on.

- **Breaking point** - at this point, the victim has no sense of belonging. They do not know who they are, what they believe in, and have no support system. Here a person might sink into depression because they are already torn away from reality. The attacker will most likely use this stage to install news beliefs in this person because he has completely forgotten his old belief system.

- **Leniency** – with the victim already depressed and needing help, the attacker approaches them as if trying to help them. The victim will feel great trust and pour his heart out to the very person that led him to this stage. The attacker will make the victim feel gratitude towards them for the small helps that they will offer during this stage.

- **The compulsion to confession** - what this step does is to make the victim open up on those things that he/she may not have previously confessed even after being cajoled into opening up. But they feel too indebted to the attacker because they are still not aware that he got them there, in the first place. So, due to their feeling of gratitude, the attacker may compel them to open up more and as a way of appreciation they will give in to their request. The attacker might also persuade them by making them believe it will be a means to let go of the possible pain.

- **Channeling of guilt** - after a long period of the victims losing their identity and carries a pang of guilt they really don't understand, and are compelled to confess, the attacker will then use their confession to make them feel guilty again. This time, however, they are made to believe in what the attacker will term as the wrong "beliefs," the reason for what they are going through. The attacker will persuade the victim that the new belief system he has instilled into the victim is the right one. This is because the old beliefs will be made to represent the physical and mental tortures they had passed through while the new beliefs represent a new

beginning and a healing process from the previous pains.

- **Releasing guilt** - The victim is made to believe that the reason for everything they have gone through has nothing to do with them as individuals. The attacker explains to the victim that he is not to blame, but instead the system he believes in. He is therefore convinced that for him to get back to his norm again, he needs to drop anything including those people that tie him to his former beliefs syatem and adapt the new one that the attacker will offer. Depending on what the attacker intends to achieve, he will present a new order and even introduce new friends to the victim so that he cannot turn back to his old system.

- **Progress and harmony** - the victim is made to choose between one group, the victim's people, and the new people introduced by the attacker. Mostly the victim will choose the one presented by the attacker because it's not only offered as a safe means but also as a solution to all the pains the old system made him go through. Here the attacker may even stop the torturous as he invests his time into making the victim believe and love the new system. The victim is also made to feel as if by choosing this new system, they haven't done anyone any wrong.

- **Final confession and rebirth** - Here, the victim has already taken sides, and the side, in this case, means the new one. They are therefore carried through the process of initiations into the new life. It's called the rebirth because the victim has just restarted his/her life and has been convinced that the new experience is better than the previous one. They, therefore, get into the rebirth with the promise of not looking back at where they came from.

HOW NOT TO BE BRAINWASHED:

- **Knowing brainwashing styles** - the first thing that manipulators do is spot their prey, you can avoid being a target by being emotionally stable, so you are not an easy target. The manipulator will strike when the victim is most likely to be emotionally unstable. The victim might have lost their loved one, lost their job, or be going through a bad relationship break-up.

- **Being cautious** - when people approach you with suspicious motives like trying to provoke your anger or hatred towards close people in your life, it's a great sign to keep away from such people.

- **Attacks on self-esteem** - be careful of the people who want to play with your self-esteem. Those people that want to make you feel guilty and bad about yourself. People who want to take advantage of your emotions by either verbal or physical attacks are to be handled with caution.

- **Group initiations** - this is when someone is continually trying to fix you in a group that you don't seem to be likely interested in, its good to be cautious. They may be trying to trick you into getting into their group in the hopes that you will forget your world.

- **Being wary of offers** - the manipulator will try to offer you irresistible gifts or help that you may really need. Their strategy is that by doing this, the attacker earns your trust and can, therefore, get close enough to you so that they can easily manipulate you.

- **Learning the other person** - when someone offers you help, it's good to pause and ask yourself why they provided support. What will they gain from helping you, or what are their intentions? Most times, we are brainwashed because we do not take the time to learn about the other person. We trust without first questioning why we are easily trusting and therefore become weaker than the manipulator who has already done their homework with you.

- **Brainwashing** is only achieved when the manipulator is in total control of their victim's feelings. The social influence alters a person's way of thinking, and the victim is influenced into adapting to the way the manipulator wants. Therefore, for brainwashing to be effective, the impact on social influence has to be great. The victim has to respect the manipulator somehow; usually, the manipulator is someone the victim has a lot of trust in. For the victim to avoid becoming a prey, it is essential for someone to

know how to protect themselves from being
brainwashed.

It is not the strongest of the species that survives, nor the most intelligent that survives. It is the one that is most adaptable to change.

Charles Darwin

CHAPTER 11

THE PROCESS

OF

BRAINWASHING

Brainwashing refers to an attempt to change the beliefs and thoughts of others against their will. It is worth noting that in psychology, brainwashing is aimed at reforming the spheres of an individual. In other words, brainwashing reforms one's mind. Art transforms the social life of an individual and causes them to change their attitudes and beliefs. One of the arts that are used in brainwashing is persuasion. One of the aspects of persuasion is that it causes one to change what they think. The primary aim is to alter one's mindset and beliefs. It is worth noting that brainwashing uses three approaches, which include education, compliance, and persuasion. Education (or rather, propaganda) allows people to change their beliefs on what they initially believed in. The art focuses on social influence and the mindset of an individual.

PREPARATION

The art of brainwashing uses several strategies to be effective. One of the techniques that has much been used is the art of persuasion. In persuasion, one identifies an idea that needs to be instilled in people's minds. It is worth noting that you can't just introduce a new idea into a person's life and expect them to follow without questioning anything. However, if persuasion is effectively used, a person may be easily brainwashed and starts believing in those new ideas. Thus, it is wise to prepare the aspect of persuading someone into believing in something new. One of the best things to do is to understand what they think categorically. For instance, some cults have brainwashed people in terms of their religion. The first thing that the leaders of these cults do is to learn what other people believe. Then, they identify the weakness of what other people believe in and start working on it. The weakness act as a loophole where such leaders use to start the process of brainwashing their followers. They are always enticing, and they promise of greater things ahead. Such leaders have lovely words that are vital in persuading people to think or to believe in other things they usually would not.

VULNERABLE CONDITION

One of the aspects that persuaders use to win the confidence of those who choose to listen to them is the art of identifying one's weakness. In other words, if you are in a vulnerable condition, there are chances that you don't believe in everything you know. In other words, you might be in a fragile state and might be tossed from one point to the other. The persuaders or leaders of cults use such vulnerability to introduce other things as well as beliefs that seem to be enticing. For instance, a cult may cover all the expenses that one uses as they travel to their worship centers. In the villages, there might be people who are vulnerable and die from visiting town centers. In such cases, they might be

swayed up by this cult and end up believing in other beliefs.

THE ELEMENTS

The art of brainwashing is more of a state of mind. Thus, a person will be introduced into new things as well as ideas irrespective of what they believe in. In other words, persuasion is a significant aspect that helps the process of brainwashing to be effective. Belief requires one to categorically engage in the process of convincing people to starts behaving or believing in new things. The other element that makes brainwashing to be useful is the art of sacrificing. In other words, one needs to sacrifice and undergo a cost for people to believe in what they know. In other words, the art of preparation and convincing people to follow the belief system you want to introduce is vital. However, with sufficient preparation, perseverance, and sacrifice, the new beliefs are introduced into people's lives hence being brainwashed.

THE LEADER

The leader of a particular cult plays a critical role in ensuring that there is adequate preparation, and the best means of persuasion are used. In other words, the leaders carry the visions and thus understand what is expected of them. In most cases, such leaders will identify the areas that need to be addressed and work in improving them. Leaders carry the weight of the matter. They are the one who introduces a particular aspect in the life of their followers. Most leaders are charismatic and sturdy. Such characters cause their followers to treat then as gods. In most cases, the leader will isolate an idea that needs to be explored and work on maximizing the benefits.

THE FOLLOWERS

Without a substantive number of followers, the art of brainwashing can't be practical. In other words, followers play a critical role in ensuring that brainstorming is complete. There is no way the process will be termed as complete without a considerable number of followers. On believing new ideas, the followers are used by the leader to increase the spread of the new cult or beliefs. The leaders also use the followers to remind others of the need to follow them by highlighting several benefits.

THE PROCESS

In most cases, the leaders, as well as the followers, use the process of persuasion to entice them into joining them. For instance, one may identify a group and plan on meeting them. In most cases, the leaders will speak confidently and sell the ideas of the cult. Persuasion is the key to the success of each activity.

In most cases, for a leader to be effective, they, in most cases, identify issues that closely affect the parties they are seeking. They will stay positive and entice their listeners with sweet words. The leader will speak of the merits of following them without considering the disadvantages. They, in most cases, use the process of arresting the minds of their listeners and urge them on the need to take a particular route or believe in one specific aspect of life. Thus, persuasion and team building are one of the primary processes that are used to enhance effective persuasion.

CHAPTER 12

CASE STUDIES OF

DARK PSYCHOLOGY:

JOSEPH STALIN,

ADOLF HITLER,

AND

CHARLES MANSON

As outlined earlier, dark psychology is the study of human condition, as it relates to the psychological nature of people to prey upon others. If one compares the three persons, one may think that one person is different for the other. Stalin is known for his notorious nature of killing a lot of people. Manson, on the other, is the least of the three personnel. Hitler, on the other hand, was able to achieve his goals via thriving arts. This chapter will thus involve a detailed discussion of the three of them.

ADOLF HITLER

Adolf Hitler came from an average middle-class family who had money issues. They used to suffer like any other family during the early twentieth century. He started his reign after World War 1 that led to the emergence of a racist version in Germany. One of the aspects that are well known for Hitler is that he lived in a state of depression as well as embarrassment. Thus, his later words were always comforting. In other words, he was described as a master of rhetoric and left the crowd he spoke to sitting in awe following his speech. One of the critical aspects is that he used to speak from his heart and gained a large following in the long run. He used to say what the listeners needed to hear as Hitler knew what suffering was. The people in Germany thus offered him support, and he became a charismatic leader. Besides the fact that he gained more power, love, and trust from different people, he used his talent in a much darker agenda. In other words, he used it to kill people and eliminate the unwanted population. He used to achieve this via camps, schooling as well as propaganda. Through his actions as well as persuasion techniques, he made people feel as if they are doing well. He was effective in persuading his troops such that they used to kill a mass of people, and yet they won't feel any sense of guilt.

JOSEPH STALIN

One aspect that is well known about Josef Stalin is that he was very selective of the topics he talked about. He was, however, very persuasive such that after speaking with his audience, he would ensure that he has persuaded the people listening to him and make them behave or think the way he wanted. Stalin also used rhetoric to appeal to his working class. One of the aspects that is critical about his speech is that he instilled fear due to his power. Thus, all who listened to him were persuaded and would not question or argue with

him. He was different from other people in the sense that he didn't feel guilt even after convincing his audience to act

accordingly. The other aspect of Stalin is that he used to punish people over issues not explained.

For instance, if one made a mistake, he or she would be summoned by his officers, and no explanations made. The guards of his troops would act like Hitler. In other words, they would treat other people brutally and feel no sense of humanity in them. They would kill a mass of people and followed their conviction without considering the guilt therein or the losses they caused. One aspect that made Stalin more compelling is the fact that the Soviet Union was looking for a strong leader. Although he was not perfect, one of the elements that made Stalin to be preferred by the Union was that he has appetizing words. He would speak, and everyone in the society would love to listen to his encouraging words. He gave people hope and persuaded them in such a way that people felt that there are no other means of escaping from their issues apart from the methods offered by Stalin.

CHARLES MANSON

One thing that makes Charles fit into this case study is that he wasn't a leader of any nation and had no background of leadership qualities. However, he was able to get a family and attract a massive following in the long run. He was persuasive in the sense that he caused people to murder other people from being a part of his cult. At a point, there were more than 100 people who joined his cult. Charles used to persuade these people using religion alongside the environment they were living in. The other aspects that made him more persuasive are the fact that he used drugs as well as euphoria and love to make people feel good. His compelling nature led people to kill. However, he was able to use tactics that attracted a massive following among the people. The drugs and free love he used to offer to his followers made them kill and act appropriately, yet they never felt any sense of insecurity or guilt.

It is worth noting that all three persons had one thing in common. They persuaded their followers to do things that they would not do when they were sober. For instance, Charles used to give drugs to his followers and caused them to kill others without a second thought. Also, Hitler has been brought up in a devastating state, and he knew what suffering was. Thus, he was an eloquent speaker and persuasive as well. He used to persuade other people over the things he desired in life. He, therefore, used his persuasive tactics to eliminate the unwanted population in Germany as a way of revenge for the sufferings he experienced. He used his troops to kill the Jews who had settled in Germany mercilessly. Stalin, on the other hand, was very persuasive using his enticing words. One of the aspects that made him influential is the fact that he came at a time when the Soviet Union wanted a leader. Stalin gained popularity following the fact that he was persuasive and had attracted a large following. However, he was able to effectively manipulate his followers and used them to perform merciless kicking as well as punish innocent people.

CHAPTER 13

BRAINWASHING TRICKS THAT WORK WITH ANYONE, EVEN THE SMARTEST

To any average person, brainwashing is associated with a cult or form of witchcraft, but this is not usually the case. Nowadays, there are a ton of ways that people are brainwashed on a day-to-day basis without even knowing. Have you ever asked yourself why many movements that do not typically stand for any critical cause tend to have many followers? If you thought of brainwashing, then you might be on to something. The thought of brainwashing an individual can seem like a technical undertaking that requires a ton of expertise, but in the real sense, it is a much subtle art that many individuals and corporations have mastered. There is a lot of brainwashing tricks that can, without a doubt, work on any individual.

SUBLIMINAL BRAINWASHING IN FILMS

A lot of individuals are big fans of movies, and they watch them on a day-to-day basis. All these movies have certain plots that mostly involve the good guys and the bad guys. Blockbuster movies like The Lord of the Rings, Harry Potter, and The Matrix all have a similar plot involving a rivalry between the good guys and the bad guys. One interesting thing is that in all these films, the bad guys are portrayed as beasts or aliens who are eventually defeated in the battle of good versus the bad. After watching these films, you are automatically programmed, without knowing, to have a negative impulse towards foreign creatures as they are made out to be evil in these films. If you happen to meet one in real life, your first instinct would be to kill them or run for your life because that is what the movies have told you. You will not take a minute to question whether the creature is actually a threat to your safety or not. There are also many movies involving snakes that attack individuals and unleash terror on innocent civilians. After watching such a movie, the first thing you will do when you see a snake, whether it is resting or minding its own business is to kill it because the movies you have watched have made you believe that the only things snakes do is attack people. This clearly a subtle form of brainwashing that even a smart person will fall victim of.

SENSE OF BELONGING

Another trick involves preying on the need for a sense of belonging to various individuals. Humans are social beings, and as social beings, we all seek a sense of belonging to make us feel secure, wanted, and accepted by the people around us.

After going through very traumatizing ordeals like the loss of a loved one, many people tend to struggle to find a sense of belonging. Such people tend to look for other individuals who are going through similar circumstances to relate with. When an individual is in such a state, he or she is highly susceptible to brainwashing by a particular individual or group that knows how to manipulate them during their current emotional instability. Such a person will, therefore, tend to

only socialize with those individuals who he or she believes have the ability to understand them and give them a sense of belonging.

REPETITION AND REPROGRAMMING

Repetition is also a major form of brainwashing trick that not many individuals are aware of. It is the repetition of one particular affirmation, chant, or incantation over and over that eventually becomes a belief which will, with time, become a conviction. This is quite apparent in the music and entertainment industry. There are thousands if not millions of songs that are released every year, but some tend to outshine others in a surreal way. You will find that a particular song is being played in every particular radio station or to the station and even though you did not like it at first, you slowly become fond of it. This repetition engrains the song in the subconscious mind that eventually makes you think you like the song when in the real sense, you don't.

Another example is how the mainstream media endorses a certain genre of music and makes it seem like it is the coolest thing to listen to. You eventually also find yourself favoring that type of music and ignoring other genres because you have been brainwashed to think that is what you are supposed to be listening to. Repeating your opinion makes people believe it no matter how stupid it is. This is one thing that, sadly, you could have guessed if you followed politics or talks on the radio. Say it enough, and people will believe it— for example, how many of you think Al Gore claims to have invented the Internet? He said no such thing, but pundits and comedians repeated it enough that it became true. It's the same reason anti-vaccination zealots are sticky to their guns, even while they cause diseases to spread like wildfire. They "heard" vaccines were dangerous, and that's literally all it takes, hearing it over and over. Even if the source is a total stranger, it's just the way human social behavior works—if a message is repeated enough times, others will begin to accept it as a commonly held belief in the group. In fact, studies have found that if just one persona repeats the same opinion three times, it has a whopping 90 percent chance of converting three different people in the group to have the same opinion. That's how both politics and conspiracy theories work, isn't it? But what makes it so treacherous is the fact that all it takes to sway people's beliefs is one crazy person. It doesn't even work all that well with multiple people. A study on the phenomenon exposed one group to an opinion repeated by three different people, another to that same opinion repeated by one-person multiple times. Incredibly, the group subjected to one single guy repeating the opinion was three times more susceptible to changing their own opinions than the others. Even when we actively register that, it's just one person's opinion; we're still likely to believe it.

IMITATION

Imitation is also a brainwashing trick that not many individuals are aware of. If you work in a profession where tips make up a significant portion of your income, it's crucial that your customers see you as a pleasant enough person to well, tip. It's good luck, then, that it's entirely possible to use a simple repeated word trick to sway people in your favor, to the point where they're way more likely to give you money. All you need to do is repeat the last few words they said and generally behave in a pleasant manner. And it is actually part of a broader set of techniques that every politician and con artist knows. You can bring people to your side and get them to do things for you just by imitating them. Humans are social animals, and we all have a switch that flips in our brain that says, "This person is like me; I should help them." In one study, they found that customers were more likely to buy from salespeople who repeated phrases they used or their mannerisms. It doesn't even have to be verbal. In another experiment, if the researcher mimicked the posture and body language of the subject, the subject was three times as likely to help him pick up a box of pens he'd dropped. This study explored the relationship between mimicry and generous tips. They first went into a restaurant and calculated an average tip; then, they told the server to repeat what half of her customers said after ordering, exactly as they said it. With the other half, she would simply say what servers normally say. The tips from mimicked customers were whopping 68 percent more generous than those from the non-mimicked ones. Regardless of factors like the accuracy of the order and wait time, just hearing their words repeated back to them put them in a more positive state of mind.

USE OF RITUALS

A human being is a creature of ritual and habit, even and especially when it comes to food. When it's your birthday, the cake tends to come to the tune of a discordant, unenthusiastic

"Happy Birthday." If you're the religious type, chances are you precede your meals with a little prayer you give to your deity of choice before chowing down. There are all sorts of cultural reasons for that stuff, but there's a very neat magic trick these chants are able to pull off: they make whatever you're about to ingest taste better. If you're not into saying grace before mealtime or the very first bars of "Happy Birthday" send you into a murderous frenzy, pretty much any quirky ritual will die. Mutter, "Petri Piper picked a peck of pickled peppers," three times under your breath while grinning widely and eyeballing the couple at the next table. Stand on your head and loudly scream, "I dedicate this meal to Sakami, the god of turmoil and madness. It doesn't seem to matter, as long as you do it. This is a subtle form of brainwashing that tunes the mind to think whatever you are going to eat will taste better.

CHAPTER 14

DARK TRIAD

If only everyone in this world were morally upright and

virtuous, then there would be no places built as cells, courts, and prisons. However, it is human nature always to want to accomplish some goals. Sometimes, you feel that you would achieve something if only your colleagues would not stand in your way. What results is jealousy, violence,

murder, or another vice—and this results in the society being filled with competition, war, and immorality.

You cannot define the real dark triad that one is suffering from, as they may have more than one personality disorder. However, at some rates, this condition is treatable by addressing the negative behaviors of that person. Therefore, encourage them that they are not the only ones suffering, highlight some of the repercussions of those behaviors, and finally, help them to change.

HOW TO IDENTIFY DARK TRIAD TRAITS

Sometimes, it is tough to notice someone experiencing that personality disorder. At some rates, you will judge them harshly. It is good to know early if your child or beloved is experiencing these disorderly symptoms for therapeutic nursing. Otherwise, do not blame yourself if your colleague is put in handcuffs when you should have done something to save him or her. It is essential to learn the characteristics found in them to identify the victim. The following are some of those characteristics.

These people are mostly manipulative. In this sense, it means that they always want to influence you to do something that benefits them and not you. They feel that your presence inhibits their operations, and they will scheme in various ways to get you out of the picture. Some of them possess emotional intelligence where they will blackmail you and correct you.

They do not care about your feelings and wishes. That means they only live for themselves. They consider you as their servant, what your desire is nothing compared to theirs. They are relatively full of pride in themselves and do not like to involve others in their lives.

Lying is the best part of them because they will speak deceit against you. It is also a way of manipulating you, where they take advantage of your weakness and entice you with untrue stories. Beware of those liars because they can con you to get a business interest. Always try to learn the signs to identify when one is cheating.

As much as they lie, sometimes they nourish such sentiments with a flowery language. So, that sweet-talking person in your neighborhood, be careful with them. They quickly identify your soft spot and utilize their chances to the maximum.

They tend to want others to admire them. Sometimes, they award themselves untrue characters that are admirable in society. You may find a person who pretends to be that queen bee so that she can create attention. They hate anyone who competes or is likable more than them. They may even eliminate such a person for their gain.

CHAPTER 15

WHAT IS THE

DARK TRIAD?

"Ooh, that kid is always on the wrong; he will probably grow to be a malicious person." Such may be the remarks of a teacher tired of disciplining a child. Scholars may tell you that just by looking at the character of a person, they can identify whether that child is malicious or not. At some rate, this is true because actions speak louder than words. If you find a kid always on the wrong end—like being naughty, scornful, arrogant, and bullies' other toddlers—you can conclude that he is a dark triad fellow. However, this might not be true because some people do mature and change.

Such traits can only be found with dark triad people. They mostly show characteristics of narcissism, Machiavellianism, and psychopathy. All these traits have some things in common, which are arrogance, jealousy, selfishness, feelings of isolation, irritability, and antisocial behavior. If you find such features in fellows, know that they may be suffering from a dark triad disorder, which is harmful—that is, to say, dark triad leads to many vices of murder, rape, violence, theft, and other notable crimes.

CAUSES OF THE DARK TRIAD

If you have to learn about something, first determine the cause of that thing. It is not different from the dark triad, which is mainly related to the evilness in society. Some of these behaviors are learned or natural. There are causes of this vices that scientist tries to explain which includes.

The first one is the biological cause. Dark triad owes its roots from the genetic makeup of a person. Such traits can be carried out throughout your genes and shapes you into that person you are today. Take examples of violent parentages or families. You will surely find even the children of that person to be wicked too. In early times people believed iniquities like witchcraft and sorcery were inheritable to the offspring. Even right now, curses are considered to run down to descendants of that particular person.

The environmental factors are anther causative element of these evils. The environment means the elements that surround you. Whether is your societal teachings, values, backgrounds, or your upbringing? You may develop a narcissistic, Machiavelli's, or psychopathy traits out of what you learn from society. A child raised in wealth and those from poor backgrounds may not relate well. If you are classy, then you can develop the narcissistic attitude of a feeling of high self-worth and pride. If you are raised from humble beginnings, you surely feel jealous of your wealthy colleague and can become a thief, conman, or a criminal.

Sometimes, the experience of a person is another source of the dark triad. The things you do mostly fail to act as provocative issues in life. Therefore, if you are tasked with the same stuff again, you will develop a dark side to mitigate that lousy feeling you felt earlier. Some people are strict and angry with someone who tells them to do something they once failed. You find that most rape victims hate the child they bear out of that assault and can even mistreat them as a means of punishing the man who did that heinous act.

Other causes are the disorders one is suffering. What makes people fear to visit a mental clinic, probably you are afraid that those people will harm you. A mental disorder can cause a person to be harmful and wicked. Those suffering from depressions or chronic diseases may opt to kill other family members or commit suicide.

MACHIAVELLIANISM

"Politics is a dirty game." Such are remarks that most people usually make. This is identifiable with politicians because, oftentimes, they are deceitful and manipulative. They will come to you with flowery promises that are attractive to the ears. They will influence you into voting them, and as soon as they garner your votes, some of them will disappear into thin air. Hey, this is not about politics; it is about the Machiavellian people who are influential and focused on their interests. They, as conmen do, will manipulate you to do something for their interests. They will try to be the dominant force and will coerce you to do what they like. Some of this behavior is mainly found in dictatorial leadership.

These characters are guided by the notion that the "ends justify the means." Hence, they are not good at following routines or rules. However, they see their way of doing things as the better way. You cannot instruct them otherwise, as they will disobey you and disrespect your work protocols. If you find such mangers in the job scenario, do not be a threat to their reputation—else, you stand a chance of being sacked by them.

CHARACTERISTICS OF MACHIAVELLIAN INDIVIDUALS

They show the attitude of self-interest. These individuals are ambitious and passionate about how they will develop their public image. They are also convicted by competing with the elite and coming out victorious in a particular competition. Pursuing your talents and abilities to favor their interests is another thing they like. They like interacting with people they feel can help in their quest. Not that they love you very much, but because of your talent and after they exploit you unfairly, they will throw you away like a piece of paper.

They seem confident and charming in most cases. This scenario indicates how they will approach you in a sweet-talking manner. You will find them amusing and friendly. Sometimes, they aim to compromise your stronghold and recognize your weakness. Assertiveness and brevity are other features associated with these individuals. They speak with a "rod of iron', where they want to captivate that fear in you. You will, therefore, do as they ask due to that phobia.

They are characterized by lacking values and principles. They believe they are better than anyone; hence, your rules and principals are not their concerns. Behind the scenes, they will manipulate you to break the rules and hide when things get too bad for you—they believe their personal way of doing things is better than your means of operation.

They have these negative feelings about strangers or others and is followed by initial distrust of your ways of doing things. That means they are cynical where they easily doubt the prominence of one. However, perfect or talented you are, they will always look for a loophole to criticize you. If you go to them with a business idea, they will try to criticize it however pleasant it seems.

They tend to use flattering language upon their victims. Skills in aligning their ideologies against yours are something of their value. That flowery language they will tell you, is so sweet to refuse. They will first command you, then compliment you and align their interests in a way that you easily fall to that trick.

IT IS A DOUBLE PLEASURE TO DECEIVE THE DECEIVER.

NARCISSISM

Sometimes, we experience dealing with people who are so full of themselves. In some situations, we find people who always want things done their ways. They will claim that their approach to their doing things is perfect, and your methods have flaws and would lead to failure. Such people are egocentric and will not accept their own errors. They, therefore, justify their error. Dealing with such people is sometimes hectic, and as a result, it has led to many broken marriages. This condition persists to become a disorder.

CHARACTERISTICS OF NARCISSISTS

Some people want to look superior. They like sentiments and praises that show them how excellent they are. When you bring up something interesting, they will quickly ridicule you. They feel that their preferences should be the significant priority of that engagement. They like dominating in any conversation. They may use jargon to show that they have much knowledge over you. If they think you have a good idea, they always want to make it look like it was their original thinking.

They often rule out their failures and blame it on you. In the event of a misunderstanding, they will rampantly remind you of your recent failures. That is a scheme to put pressure on you and make you feel guilty. Most notably, when someone is guilty, you are likely to follow what they desire. In the event, it will make them feel valued. By blaming you, you will look dismal, and they will appear like they are always right.

They like praising themselves. This element shows that these narcissists' main aim is to feel valued and honored. What follows is critiques and insults on that person who is not crediting their achievements. Their thirst for power is further portrayed by them wishing to gain diplomacy.

Narcissistic typically show a sense of envious attitude. They will identify that fellow who is prosperous than them and try to compete. Therefore, they will try to criticize their competitors and even justify that your success was a result of their own doing. To criticize such projects or explain that such achievement was the result of their own doing. Some may even demolish your reputation by slandering or saying wrong about you.

Those individuals demonstrate a paranoia attitude. They always experience an irrational fear of what is going to happen next to them. They are cynical and have that distrust of people, especially strangers. If they see potential in you of being successful, they will fear that you will defeat them. Therefore, they will develop a scheme of how to put you down.

They always expect special treatment. These fellows view themselves as valuable and see it wrong if you do not recognize their eminence. They assume that every helpful service must be rendered or offered to them without question. These Narcissists feel proud of their life and attribute their fortunes as a result of their excellent doing.

Most are characterized by being conversation interrupter. That is where the narcissistic fellows feel the conversation ought to be readdressed to their ideas. They will immediately interrupt you if you talk of issues that are of their less concern to them. They will not yield to any accounts you give regarding their fiascos.

PSYCHOPATHY

CHARACTERISTICS OF PSYCHOPATHS

You are most likely to fall into their trap because of their charming nature. They will act innocent when you face them. They talk to you and treat you warmly. They hide that mask under a pretense that you hardly realize. You always feel good if you intermingle with them; however, when they strike, you will be engrossed in suffering.

How would you judge a person who, even after serving a lifetime jail time, is still not remorseful? You are, therefore, allowed to call such person a psychopath. These individuals have no regrets about their crimes. They can laugh and irritate you when you are hurting, which is painful. They perceive that whatever they do is in their best interests. How on earth can they say sorry while they are arrogant to say so?

These fellows are antisocial, as they believe that no one suits their style of living. That means they live in isolation, which involves no one. It is like they have a world of their own. If you try to force yourself on them, they will use you to their advantage or even hurt you. This element is what makes a psychiatrist diagnose them of a personality disorder. You can know why an antisocial being has no buddies and is spiteful.

You will feel terrible if you try to win their sympathy and affection. Try to wrong these people, and they will hurl you with endless insults. They are temperamental, and it is hard to appease them when they are enraged. They usually do not understand your inner desires and feelings. That means they are not empathetic and understanding. You are likely to suffer under their assault if you continue that relationship or marriage.

These people are active in sex life. They are characterized by being sexually sensitive. Therefore, they manipulate many partners to do favors for them. Moreover, they cannot settle in a long-term marriage but chooses many mates for this pleasure. Preference of a shorter relationship rather than the long-term relationship is what they are mostly attributed to.

Look into the depths of your own soul and learn first to know yourself, then you will understand why this illness was bound to come upon you and perhaps you will thenceforth avoid falling ill.

When making a decision of minor importance, I have always found it advantageous to consider all the pros and cons. In vital matters, however, such as the choice of a mate or a profession, the decision should come from the unconscious, from somewhere within ourselves. In the important decisions of personal life, we should be governed, I think, by the deep inner needs of our nature.

Sigmund Freud

CPSIA information can be obtained
at www.ICGtesting.com
Printed in the USA
BVHW010810010321
601200BV00018B/106